5 principles applicable for a Perfect leadership

How to lead and rule under pressure with courage

Roy L. McVay

5 principles

How to lead and rule under pressure

Copyright © by **Roy L. McVay** 2024. All rights reserved.

Before this document is duplicated or reproduced in any manner, the publisher's consent must be gained. Therefore, the contents within can neither be stored electronically, transferred, nor kept in a database. Neither in Part nor full can the document be copied, scanned, faxed, or retained without approval from the publisher or creator.

5 principles

Table of Content

Introduction

Chapter 1

Chapter 2

Chapter 3

Chapter 4

Chapter 5

Introduction

In a world where traditional notions of leadership no longer hold sway, Roy L. McVay offers a compelling and transformative perspective in "How to lead and rule under pressure." Through years of research and working with leaders across diverse industries, Brown reveals that true leadership isn't about titles or wielding power; it's about having the courage to recognize and develop the potential in people and ideas.

5 principles

In "How to lead and rule under pressure," Roy L. McVay challenges the status quo by emphasising the importance of curiosity, vulnerability, and empathy in leadership. Roy L. McVay demonstrates that by embracing these traits, leaders can foster authentic connections, drive innovation, and navigate challenges with resilience and integrity.

Drawing from real-world examples and practical insights, Roy L. McVay presents a roadmap for cultivating daring leadership in any organisation. Roy L. McVay explores the essential skill sets that define courageous leadership and provides

5 principles

actionable strategies for embedding a culture of courage and empowerment.

Whether you're a seasoned leader seeking to reignite your passion for leadership or an aspiring leader eager to make a meaningful impact, "How to lead and rule under pressure" offers invaluable guidance and inspiration. It's a rallying cry for individuals and organisations alike to embrace vulnerability, connect authentically, and lead with courage in an ever-evolving world.

Chapter 1

Redefining Leadership in the 21st Century

In today's rapidly evolving world, the traditional definition of leadership no longer holds true. Leadership is no longer confined to those with titles or formal authority; it's about embracing a mindset of responsibility and empowerment. Roy L. McVay's groundbreaking research reveals that anyone can be a leader by recognizing and nurturing the potential within themselves and others.

5 principles

The Startup Innovator

Consider the story of Sarah, a young entrepreneur who founded a tech startup in her garage. Without a prestigious title or decades of experience, Sarah embarked on her journey by recognizing the untapped potential in her team and ideas. She fostered a culture where every member felt valued and empowered to contribute their unique skills and perspectives. Through her visionary leadership, Sarah transformed her fledgling startup into a thriving

5 principles

company, disrupting the industry and inspiring others to follow suit.

The Community Organizer

Imagine Juan, a passionate community organiser in a small town. Despite lacking formal authority, Juan took it upon himself to address pressing issues facing his community. He rallied neighbours together, recognizing their collective potential to create positive change. By empowering individuals to take ownership of their community's future, Juan demonstrated that

5 principles

leadership is not about titles but about taking responsibility and inspiring others to action.

Roy L. McVay's research challenges us to rethink our assumptions about leadership and embrace a new paradigm where everyone has the capacity to lead. By fostering a culture of empowerment and accountability, we can unlock the full potential of individuals and organisations, driving innovation, and positive change in the world.

Chapter 2

The Power of Vulnerability in Leadership

In this chapter, we explore the transformative role of vulnerability in leadership. Roy L. McVay challenges the conventional wisdom that leaders must project an image of invulnerability and certainty. Instead, Roy L. McVay argues that embracing vulnerability is essential for building authentic connections, fostering trust, and driving meaningful change.

5 principles

The Corporate Executive

Meet Emily, a seasoned corporate executive leading a large team in a competitive industry. For years, Emily believed that vulnerability was a sign of weakness and strove to maintain a facade of strength and control. However, as challenges mounted and morale waned within her team, Emily realised that her unwillingness to show vulnerability was hindering their ability to connect and collaborate effectively.

Determined to change course, Emily decided to share her own struggles and uncertainties with her team during a weekly meeting. She spoke openly about the difficulties she faced in navigating the company's recent restructuring and admitted her fears about the future. To her surprise, instead of diminishing her authority, Emily's vulnerability inspired her team members to open up about their own challenges and concerns.

As they shared their experiences and supported one another, a newfound sense of camaraderie and trust emerged within the team. With barriers broken down and communication channels opened, they were able to collaborate more

5 principles

effectively, leading to innovative solutions and improved performance.

Emily's story illustrates the power of vulnerability in leadership. By embracing her own vulnerability and creating a space for others to do the same, she was able to foster a culture of authenticity and trust within her team, making success coke true in the face of adversity.

Through practical examples like Emily's, Roy L. McVay demonstrates how vulnerability can be a catalyst for connection, innovation, and resilience in leadership. By letting go of the need

5 principles

to appear invulnerable and embracing authenticity, leaders can cultivate stronger relationships and inspire greater commitment from their teams.

5 principles

Chapter 3

Cultivating Courageous Conversations

In this pivotal chapter, Roy L. McVay delves into the importance of courageous conversations in leadership. Roy L. McVay highlights how leaders can navigate difficult topics with empathy, authenticity, and integrity, fostering deeper connections and driving positive change within their teams and organisations.

The Team Conflict Resolution

5 principles

Imagine a scenario where tensions are running high within a team due to conflicting personalities and communication breakdowns. Rather than ignoring the issue or resorting to blame, the team leader, let's call her Maya, decides to initiate a courageous conversation. She gathers the team members in a safe and respectful environment and encourages each person to share their perspective openly and honestly.

As the conversation unfolds, emotions surface, and grievances are aired. Maya listens

5 principles

attentively, validating each person's experience and seeking to understand the underlying root causes of the conflict. Through active listening and empathetic communication, Maya helps the team members recognize their common goals and values, fostering a sense of unity and collaboration.

By the end of the conversation, the team members have gained a newfound appreciation for one another's perspectives and have developed strategies for resolving conflicts constructively in the future. Through Maya's leadership, what could have escalated into a toxic situation is transformed into an opportunity for growth and strengthened relationships within the team.

The Performance Feedback Session

Consider the experience of Alex, a manager tasked with delivering performance feedback to a struggling team member, let's call her Rachel. Instead of delivering the feedback in a one-sided manner, Alex approaches the conversation as an opportunity for growth and development. He begins by expressing his genuine concern for

5 principles

Rachel's well-being and career progression, setting a supportive tone for the discussion.

Throughout the conversation, Alex provides specific examples of areas where Rachel can improve, while also acknowledging her strengths and contributions to the team. He encourages Rachel to share her own perspective and challenges, creating a dialogue rather than a monologue. Together, they brainstorm actionable steps that Rachel can take to address her areas for improvement, setting clear expectations and timelines for follow-up.

5 principles

As a result of the courageous conversation, Rachel feels valued and supported by her manager, rather than criticised or demoralised. She leaves the meeting with a renewed sense of motivation and commitment to her professional development, while Alex gains insights into how he can better support his team members in their growth journeys.

Through these practical experiences, Roy L. McVay illustrates how courageous conversations can foster trust, collaboration, and growth within teams. By approaching difficult topics with empathy and openness, leaders can create spaces

5 principles

for authentic dialogue and drive positive outcomes in their organisations.

Chapter 4

The Teachable Skills of Daring Leadership

In this chapter, we introduces the four skill sets that define courageous leadership: rumbling with vulnerability, living into our values, braving trust, and learning to rise. We emphasises that these skills are not innate traits but behaviours that can be taught, practised, and mastered. Through practical examples and exercises, We empower readers to cultivate these skills and become more effective and authentic leaders.

5 principles

Rumbling with Vulnerability

Consider the experience of David, a team leader facing resistance to change within his organisation. Instead of avoiding difficult conversations or pushing through with force, David decides to rumble with vulnerability. He acknowledges the uncertainty and fear surrounding the proposed changes and openly shares his own doubts and concerns with his team.

5 principles

By creating a space for open dialogue and acknowledging the emotions at play, David fosters trust and authenticity within his team. Together, they explore the underlying reasons for resistance and collaboratively develop strategies for navigating the changes effectively. Through this process of rumbling with vulnerability, David demonstrates courageous leadership and paves the way for a more resilient and adaptable team.

Living into Our Values

5 principles

Imagine the story of Maria, a nonprofit leader committed to social justice and equality. In the face of competing priorities and limited resources, Maria is faced with a difficult decision: whether to compromise her organisation's values to secure funding from a controversial donor. Instead of succumbing to pressure, Maria chooses to live into her values with courage and integrity.

She refuses the funding offer, knowing that accepting it would compromise the mission and values of her organisation. By staying true to her principles, Maria inspires her team and

5 principles

supporters, reinforcing their trust and loyalty. Though the decision may come with short-term challenges, Maria's unwavering commitment to her values sets a powerful example of daring leadership and strengthens the foundation of her organisation for the long term.

Through these practical examples, Roy L. McVay illustrates how daring leadership involves actively engaging with vulnerability, staying aligned with our values, and building trust within teams and organisations. By mastering these teachable skills, leaders can navigate uncertainty with courage and

5 principles

authenticity, inspiring others to follow suit and driving positive change in the world.

Chapter 5

Embedding Courage in Organisational Culture

In this concluding chapter, Roy L. McVay explores how leaders can embed the value of courage in organisational culture, creating environments where vulnerability is celebrated, trust is fostered, and innovation thrives. Through practical examples and strategies, Roy L. McVay demonstrates how cultivating a culture of courage can unleash the full potential of teams and drive meaningful change.

5 principles

The Tech Startup

Consider the story of Sarah, the founder of a tech startup committed to fostering a culture of innovation and creativity. From the outset, Sarah prioritised vulnerability and transparency within her organisation, encouraging her team members to share their ideas and concerns openly. She instituted regular "courage meetings," where team members could discuss challenges and brainstorm solutions without fear of judgement.

5 principles

As a result of Sarah's leadership, the startup thrived in a competitive industry, attracting top talent and producing groundbreaking products. By embedding the value of courage in the organisation's culture, Sarah created a dynamic and inclusive environment where every team member felt empowered to contribute their unique perspectives and take calculated risks.

The Nonprofit Organization

Imagine an international nonprofit organisation dedicated to humanitarian aid and disaster relief. Under the leadership of Juan, the organisation

5 principles

prioritised courage and empathy in their approach to serving vulnerable communities around the world. Juan encouraged his team members to lean into discomfort and uncertainty, recognizing that true innovation often arises from challenging the status quo.

Through their courageous efforts, the organisation implemented new initiatives and partnerships that expanded their impact and reach. By fostering a culture of courage and collaboration, Juan transformed the organisation into a beacon of hope and resilience, inspiring

5 principles

others in the nonprofit sector to embrace bold, compassionate leadership.

Through these practical examples, Roy L. McVay illustrates how embedding courage in organisational culture can lead to innovation, resilience, and positive change. By creating environments where vulnerability is celebrated and trust is cultivated, leaders can unleash the full potential of their teams and organisations, driving progress and making a lasting difference in the world.

www.ingramcontent.com/pod-product-compliance
Lightning Source LLC
Chambersburg PA
CBHW050253230526
45470CB00005B/2247